Triumphant

Women's Inspiring Stories of Overcoming,

Working Through

and Wondering

Compiled and Edited by

Elizabeth Hash Lopina

Published by Wiltshire Books

ISBN 978-0-9831685-6-0

Printed in the United States of America

For Nicholas, Sarah and Mary Catherine

Table of Contents

Chapter Four: Learning

Chapter Six: Loss

Preface

Several years ago, while studying a book for a Bible study group I was a part of, the idea came to me to put this book together. The book we were reading included stories of finding God in everyday life and those who submitted stories were theologians, psychiatrists, noted authors and other experts in their field. Though it was a good book and I got a lot out of it, I was in a challenging place myself regarding motherhood, and I wondered what it would be like to hear stories of struggle from women I knew. I would put their stories in a similar format as the book I had been studying, but the authors would be everyday people sharing something very personal and not necessarily from their occupation or field of study.

When I had my first child I had a tough time transitioning into motherhood. My pregnancy was fine, but my son's birth was a bit dramatic. I was induced since he was a week late, but during labor his heartbeat would decrease every time I had a contraction. Since I wasn't progressing enough, the doctor thought it best, after hours on end of nothingness, that I have a cesarean section. All went well with that and I had a healthy baby boy who to this day is not to be rushed. However, I struggled with breastfeeding and ended up with a systemic infection and was almost readmitted to the hospital when my son was only a week old. I eventually healed physically, but could not shake my baby blues. Looking back, I feel certain I had undiagnosed post-partum depression.

To sound completely cliché, one day I was watching Oprah and I might have very well been eating a bon-bon (read miniature Reece's cups), and the show's guests were new mothers who also found motherhood to be a challenge and exhausting. There were also older mothers on the show who thought these women were complainers, that taking care of a child isn't that hard. Jackpot. I felt completely validated as I stared at the television listening to other women voice what I had been feeling all along. The older women had valid points. Men are a lot more hands-on today than they were when I was a baby, but come on. Nothing was hard at all? Nothing? No sleep? Colicky baby? Breastfeeding trouble? What makes some of the struggling new moms feel bad is nobody else admitting any difficulties and telling us to suck it up.

My theory on one of the reasons I was a little stressed out is that it is NOT the '70s anymore! When I was little, my mother could pay the housekeeper/babysitter minimum wage if she needed or wanted to be out of the house. Not these days. How many friends have I heard say they can't afford to volunteer because of what they would have to spend on child care? And hiring someone to clean your house? Forget about it. Life isn't like it was. I couldn't send my kids out to play when they were little because it's just not safe to do that anymore. All of this leads to a lot of…togetherness. I didn't want to make it a competition of who's generation had it tougher, I just wanted the benefit of the doubt…I was having a tough time.

I went back to work after my son was born, but soon realized the rushing around to the sitter before and after work, and the fact that my salary was barely enough to pay the sitter, didn't make my job worth the trouble. So, my husband and I decided I should leave work and stay home to care for our son. I will never question that this was the right decision for our family, but for a woman who had her first child at 30, it took a while to adjust to a paycheck of kisses, hugs and finger-paintings instead of actual money that could help pay the mounting bills. I had enjoyed freedom during my "roaring 20s," but as an extrovert who was now home a lot more with a small child, I had a nagging case of cabin fever. Even though I had babysat plenty, taking care of your own child and being ultimately responsible for this little human was at times quite daunting, and please tell me there is agreement here…mentally and physically exhausting. So, I started wondering if I was good enough. At any of it. I compared myself to other moms in every way, shape or form, feeling I often came up short. I also felt guilty for feeling this way and didn't want to share this with anyone for fear that they would think I resented or regretted having my children.

After my second child was born, I sought counseling, and if we had better insurance I would have continued seeing her to this day. It was liberating being able to tell an objective ear my thoughts and feelings and not be judged. She was there to listen and to help, and the answer I came away with after questions and doubts and comparing myself to others was another question…Who cares? That's right. Who. Cares. It was enlightening and empowering.

Of course I came away with more than that, having realized I am a good mom. I mean, I didn't always have negative feelings, I just needed help getting over the hump. I should have looked at it more practically, like a transition into any new job. There would be kinks to work out and adjustments to make. My house was not spic and span all the time, because that wasn't important to me and not how I wanted to spend my down time. My body didn't look like I wanted it to because I'm not a believer in deprivation. I knew what I needed to do and I would do it when I was ready. I didn't appear in full hair and makeup with a cute outfit on to drop off my kids at preschool because I'm not a morning person. I was setting myself up to fail with false expectations when all I had to do was realize who I really was. Eventually the fog began to lift.

Having all of those feelings of self-doubt and not wanting to admit any of it to anyone made me feel isolated and alone. The book would be a way not only to commiserate, but to share how we all got through it, and hopefully inspire and comfort other young women.

I wrote to many women friends and family members telling them what I was interested in doing and a lot of them wanted to participate. I asked for stories of inspiration, when they overcame something, learned from a mistake, struggled with an issue, or accomplished a goal. What I thought would be more stories like mine morphed into a variety of trials and tribulations I am humbled they shared with me.

These women wrote about tough choices, overcoming abuse, struggling with fertility, enduring racism, caring for dying parents, childhood illness, and many more of life's experiences and making the best of them. I treasure them all and am so grateful for all of the women who participated in this book.

My hope is that anyone who reads this book finds some sort of inspiration, that if only one person's heart is touched, one conversation is started on a touchy subject, one person finds courage to speak their truth, or begins to let go of hatred...then this book that took way too long to finally put together is totally and completely worth it.

Chapter One

Courage

"I remembered that the real world was wide,
and that a varied field of hopes and fears,
of sensations and excitements, awaited those who had the courage
to go forth into its expanse,
to seek real knowledge of life amidst its perils."

From *Jane Eyre* by Charlotte Bronte

That Still Small Voice

Growing up in a family of 6 children, I was rarely "alone." As a very talkative and social adult, and mother of 2 daughters, I again find that I am rarely "alone." In my world, alone time is sought out and cherished as if it's one of the rarest of world commodities. To come home to a peacefully quiet house and several hours of time to spend however I like has been better, at times, than any material gift I've been given. Even as a young child, I sought out the solitude of my room, the edge of the neighborhood pond at twilight, the secret enclosure created by our giant weeping willow tree. As I look back on my life, and specifically on the times when I felt torn and unsure, I realize how fortunate I've been, for I never have been truly "alone."

Growing up in a Latter Day Saint home, (to most of the population, this translates as Mormon) we had a large family and a relatively strict spiritual upbringing. Curiosity, education and experience have certainly broadened my horizons as I entered, and journeyed throughout adulthood and while I have not remained stolid in the Latter Day Saint religion, nor any organized religion, I have a deep spiritual connection. The power of prayer has never, for one moment, escaped me and for the changes it has made in my life, I am eternally grateful.

When I was around 11 years old, I was molested by a family member. Confusion and shame ruled my existence. I was unable to focus on school work, feel connected with friends and was sure that "God" had forsaken me. I prayed fervently for an answer and it came in the form of my very own voice, when one morning I chose to yell out, speak out and end the abuse for me forever. Because of this experience, I became a better, more aware mother for my own daughters and an advocate against child abuse.

Another event where that little voice gave me courage was when I was 16. My friends and I were sitting at a railroad track crossing; lights blinking and bells clanging. We could see no train and my girlfriends were convinced it was malfunctioning and had made the decision to proceed across the tracks. I believe my constant plea to heaven allowed me to hear that still, small voice of warning to wait and be patient. Seconds after I cried out for the driver to wait, an express train came barreling through the crossing at well over 50 miles an hour.

More recently, I was seeking answers about my future. My second marriage was in shambles, ending in failure and after over a year of separation and several requests for a divorce over a seven year period, I was finally moving on with my life. Luckily, I had managed to salvage a friendship with my soon-to-be ex-husband and things were good. I began dating and was shocked on New Year's Eve when my ex professed that he was still in love with me and wanted to work things out. I was in utter shock, overwhelmed with confusion and doubt. Did I want to set myself up again for that pain? Could I and should I turn away from a nine year marriage? I prayed steadily, this time not for guidance but for a flat out answer. After ten days, my husband confronted me demanding my answer. In that moment I realized that, although I had dedicated nine years to saving our marriage, I was only allowed ten days to make a life altering decision. I knew that I had my answer. It was time for me to move forward and leave that relationship behind.

What is the absolute best prayer that has been answered for me every day? What I see in the lives of my daughters, who are healthy, happy, stable and alive. Belief in the power of prayer and knowledge that we really are never alone.

Betsey Manzoni

Reach Out

I was only two months into my sobriety when a challenge faced me and I was anxious about how to overcome it. I had been living with my parents, and they were planning to go away with friends for a long weekend. Though I was working the steps of Alcoholics Anonymous, I was in an out-patient treatment program. This meant I would be left alone in the house and I didn't trust myself not to drink.

On the Wednesday before that looming weekend, I ran into a friend from AA who was telling me about how she and some friends were going to the beach for the weekend. I really wanted to go with her so I could be around other people working the steps, but knew it was rude to invite myself. While we were talking, one of the friends who was going to go on the trip called to say she couldn't make it after all. I swallowed my pride and asked my friend if I could go in her place. I told her I was really scared to stay by myself in the house because of the temptations. She started to cry. "You know, I am sure God is working in our lives right now, because I need some support, too. I would LOVE for you to come with me and my family."

I was so relieved that I would be able to spend some time with friends who were battling the same things I was and we would be able to support each other.

It was one of the most relaxing and fun weekends I'd had in a long time.

When in need, reach out. There are people who can help you, and there are people you can help, too.

Lucy

The 12 Steps of Alcoholics Anonymous

1. We admitted we were powerless over alcohol—that our lives had become unmanageable.

2. Came to believe that a Power greater than ourselves could restore us to sanity.

3. Made a decision to turn our will and our lives over to the care of God as we understood Him.

4. Made a searching and fearless moral inventory of ourselves.

5. Admitted to God, to ourselves, and to another human being the exact nature of our wrongs.

6. Were entirely ready to have God remove all these defects of character.

7. Humbly asked Him to remove our shortcomings.

8. Made a list of all persons we had harmed, and became willing to make amends to them all.

9. Made direct amends to such people wherever possible, except when to do so would injure them or others.

10. Continued to take personal inventory and when we were wrong promptly admitted it.

11. Sought through prayer and meditation to improve our conscious contact with God, as we understood Him, praying only for knowledge of His will for us and the power to carry that out.

12. Having had a spiritual awakening as the result of these Steps, we tried to carry this message to alcoholics, and to practice these principles in all our affairs.

The Twelve Steps are reprinted with permission of A.A. World Services, Inc.

I Will Be Dancing

Not long ago, my husband, Maury, and I became grandparents for the seventh time. One might think that after being present for the births of our six other grandbabies we would be old pros, but this time it was different. John David Bishop decided to come into this world just two days after the rest of his mother's family (all 24 of them) departed for a week at the beach. His mother, our daughter Lisa, was becoming a mother for the first time at the age of 38, so I insisted on staying home to "boil the water."

Unbeknownst to our family, the day before they left for the beach I received a phone call from the radiologist after he had read my recent mammogram. He told me to come in that day for an ultrasound, after which he scheduled a needle biopsy for Monday, July 9th. Everyone headed to the beach on Saturday, July 7th. Sunday morning when I returned from church there was a message from Lisa saying the baby was on the way. Lisa and Dave, her husband, live in Lexington, KY – approximately two hours away. I promptly threw things in the car and was in Lexington in plenty of time for John's birth on July 8th. It was a blessing to witness Lisa becoming a mother, something she had wanted for so long, and it was as if only she, Dave and the baby were in that delivery room.

I visited the new family at the hospital the next morning, told them I would be running errands all day and wouldn't return until that evening. I certainly did not want Lisa to know about my lump and spoil their joy. In truth, I drove back to Huntington for the breast biopsy. Afterwards, still numb and with an ice pack on my left breast, I returned to the Lexington hospital, taking flowers and balloons as if I had been running errands all day. God was with me that day for I am not usually that brave.

The Bishop family arrived home the next day and what fun we had caring for the new baby and introducing him to his two dogs and two cats. On Friday the 13th my breast surgeon called me to say that the pathology report showed I had breast cancer. My heart fell and I wondered how I would tell Lisa and the rest of my family who were in route from the beach to Lexington to meet Baby John.

Mary Bishop, the paternal grandmother, had stopped by for a visit shortly before the phone call came from my doctor. Mary is an RN and provided the positive reassurance needed at that time. I don't think it was a coincidence that she arrived when she did.

As with our other grandchildren, John's birth was a gift. For Lisa and Dave it was a dream come true. For me, it was the best medicine. A special feeling came over me and I held him against my left breast- a feeling of healing. I promised him I would dance at his wedding and I will.

I have three surgeries, chemo and radiation behind me. I have a head full of new curls and clear reports on my tests. Best of all, Maury and I have been blessed with our eighth grandchild, John's baby sister. And I am promising to dance at each grandchild's wedding.

Carol Morgan Taylor

Follow the Map

Kindergarten: I met Tommy. He couldn't see me. He could see my outline, sometimes, if the light was just right. He was different than I was.

First grade: I was put in the special reading group. We had to read books with big words. A lot of big words.

Second grade: It was explained to me why a family friend my age, my peer, wasn't able to do the same things that came so easily to me. Why he sometimes stared off into space. Why his body and brain didn't cooperate. Bradley.

Third grade: I had a "big test" and got to go to the AIG (academically or intellectually gifted) room. I, too, was different.

Fourth grade: Ms. Ward entered my world and taught me how to type and read Braille. I learned about school budget cuts and how much work is involved in the everyday. I could now type papers in Braille to go home with Tommy. His mom told my mom how much she appreciated me. When the "compliment" was passed on to me I thought it was silly, he was my buddy.

Fifth grade: Tommy and I got a new buddy- Jeri. I typed a lot of Braille that year.

Sixth grade: I started to babysit my peer. I saw seizures in their full glory. I saw the look on a tired mom's face.

Then we moved. Where did everyone go? Everyone different, where did they all go? I joined every civic club, volunteered to be a part of every special community event. I found them. We all grew together but separated.

High school: Those teachers. The ones that got me, they knew I saw the world through different lenses. Not rose-colored, but different. It was also in high school when the comments started, "You should be a special education teacher." It came so often I had a rote response, "I don't have the energy."

I know who I am and I am not a teacher. I am a doer. I am happy to be a doer for those who can't or don't have the means to do for themselves. A teacher I am not.

College: I met him, that young man who swept me off my feet. That love, that relationship that changed my whole idea of what my future would be. Ken Burns lucked out because his female competition was out of the race. (My goal was to document the people of the world, to show everyone that we all are different, yet all so very similar.) Exposure. Water, land and invisible lines may separate us all, but we are all much more alike than we recognize in our day to day.

Marriage: I set the ground rules from day one. I didn't know what kind of wife I would be, but I sure knew what I wouldn't be. I wouldn't be the sole housekeeper, laundry doer, cook, toy picker upper, accountant or handyperson. I was A-Okay with 12-hour work days and with my AM radio, no power steering, and no air conditioning on a ridiculously long commute. I saw us, giving of our time and energy to help those that needed it. Great stewards of all things civically minded just because it is the right thing to do. I had the confidence we could do "it" all. Conquer the world, and if not conquer it we would sure make it a better place, just the two of us.

Baby Boy: A wonderful, easy, and downright pleasant pregnancy (as pleasant as being pregnant can be.) Childbirth, most unpleasant. My word! The end result is worth every moment of discomfort! Mothering, I knew what I would do. I knew what kind of man my son would grow up to be.

Maternity leave: Something is not right. Something is not going according to plan. The baby book I had to have? The Pooh Bear with all of the milestones listed so I just have to fill in the blanks? Both went in the trash. What have I done wrong? Have I failed him already? Doctor, please! Doctor, please help me help him! I have seen every doctor in this practice! PLEASE!

Head, shoulders, knees and toes: That is where our story really began. My son's 18-month check-up was scheduled with the head pediatrician, the one who started the practice. What happened during that appointment did it. It was the tipping point for us. My son couldn't point to his head, shoulders, knees, or toes. He couldn't point to anything. Anything. The doctor didn't know what to do with us. I was quickly labeled "that mom" expecting her son to do more than every other little boy ("You know boys can take longer to mature, you know this, right?" I was told repeatedly) I was driving them crazy.

Our next appointment was with the newest pediatrician in the practice. He flipped back through my little guy's chart and pulled out all of my concerns. He was my angel that day. In 10 minutes he had everything set up for us. He paved the way. Finally a path, a light. I wanted to hug his neck; I wanted to cry tears of joyful hope and tears of frustration that it took so long.

He patiently and sincerely explained to me the long period of time it would take to find answers (if there were answers to be found) and at the same time gave me names and numbers, resources and lists of what to do in the meantime. I was overjoyed!

Then it happened, I had to explain the "who, what, when, where and most importantly the WHY" of it all. Luckily, some of the questions were easily answered. While the '**why**'- Fragile X Syndrome, FXS, the leading known cause of inherited mental retardation, the '**who**'- my genes, and the '**when**'- well we all know how babies are made, were manageable, the '**what**' is forever changing. What it means for him, for me, for our family, and for our community, did not have an easy answer.

The world of acronyms: So it began. Three and four letter terms that flowed from the lips of trained professionals who had spent their lives filling their brains with these things that I had never even heard of, even with all of my "exposure" to the world of my peers with SN(Special Needs.) PDD-NOS, SPD, PT, OT, ST, the list goes on and on. Boggled the mind. It took so long to get the ball rolling, but once it did it felt more like an avalanche than a gentle snowfall.

IEPs: Individualized Education Plans. AH HA! This is how this school thing works…or doesn't. I am not a teacher, I am a doer. What do I DO!?!

Baby Girl: My lovely miracle baby. She was growing in my womb as I was trying to decipher this world full of acronyms, appointments, and fathom a future for my son. She entered this world while my brain decided to go for its own Grand Mal seizure debut. Just a few days after her arrival she was as healthy as could be, and I was living in an anticonvulsant medication fog. I couldn't stand with enough stability to hold her. I couldn't be left alone. My family of four temporarily included three individuals with varying degrees of need for around the clock care. She was tested. She too had Fragile X Syndrome. Here we go again.

Google: A lifesaver. No more university lending libraries for books. Access to information was a click away, as quick as dial up could handle. Much of the information could be filtered through quickly to my now trained eye. I avoided scam cures for my children. I relied on what I viewed as hard facts. I relied on what I knew to get through the days. I relied on those that I was able to connect with all over the world through the community of specialists eager to learn more, parents yearning to connect, educators, and parents turned educators charging forward!

Routines: Expected. Daily, hourly.

I never thought I would be a mom. But, when I found out I was pregnant, I saw my future as a soccer mom, minivan driver, hosting and taking kids to birthday parties and sleepovers, going to shopping malls, and theme parks. What I didn't envision was seeing my children heartbroken that they never got invited to birthday parties or sleepovers. I didn't envision physical therapy, occupational therapy, speech therapy, play therapy, music therapy, orthopedics, cardiologists, and special needs sports teams with "Buddies." I didn't envision my own children participating in Special Olympics, trying to find a church that my child is actually welcome to attend, not knowing what my child ate for lunch in 5th grade because they can't tell me, not knowing how my child got scratches and bruises on them because they can't tell me, not trusting my child alone with anyone but me, because they can't tell me anything, knowing my child will never live alone, and fearing what will happen to them when I am no longer there, and knowing the burden my child will have on friends and family for the rest of their lives, because I won't live forever…it is my life as a mom that I never dreamed I would live.

<u>Revelation</u>: I was being prepared my whole life for my children. There is no doubt in my mind.

I know that somewhere there is a little boy or girl meeting their Tommy, Bradley or Jeri. There is a Ms. Ward making an impact on someone somewhere. There is a young person gaining exposure, growing to be another Ms. Ward. There is a mom sending her child to babysit for the neighbor child who may just be a little different.

The great big world is smaller than we often realize. So maybe I did accomplish a goal I thought I lost with marriage and motherhood. Exposure. While we are all different, we are so much alike. Water, land, and invisible lines may very well separate us all. And yet, we all have dreams, hopes, and life experiences that make us who we are, who we will grow to be.

I was given a map to help me on my journey. My journey has taken me through unexpected territory, but it is not uncharted. I just had to slow down, acknowledge the legend, use my compass, and learn to ask for directions.

Heather Tolbert Lopina

The "Long and Winding Road"

I loved my job as the Director of Performing Arts. To me it was the best job in the world…teaching a craft I have been involved with all my life and cared for deeply. I was the director of the theatre program at a university and always believed great theatre changes lives and, for those who participate, creates deep and long-lasting relationships while cooperating on a project with many moving parts and many skill sets.

However, after working at this institution for 23 years, things started to fall apart. Some things were my fault, some were not, and sadly my career there ended with me taking an early retirement.

I had been in Alcoholics Anonymous for 15 years but had begun to fall off the wagon. And, though drinking was never cited in my reviews, the administration was made aware of my drinking at a cast party where there had also been underage drinking. It was then that I was "asked" to retire after 23 years of loyal service.

I was flooded with grief and sadness as I dealt with these circumstances as well as the loss of my mother during that time. She was my best friend.

I was thrown into a deep depression and considered suicide for a long, long time. My husband is a Vietnam Veteran and one day I found his service revolver in our house. I went to Bass Pro Shop and bought the bullets. I had, as I describe it now, a very romantic relationship with suicide. I planned when and where and revised my full plan over and over. I wrote many, many letters to my two boys, and also wrote out my final wishes and detailed how my husband could handle all of them.

Then, I remembered my girlfriend, Sherry, telling me how her father had committed suicide and that 30 years later she is still dealing with the emotional trauma of it. How could I put my family through that? The thought of what my boys and my husband would have to face kept me from following through that day.

22

While visiting my sister in South Carolina, still in my depression, I walked down her long and winding road toward the expressway late one night without her knowing. I contemplated what to do for a while, and then, I stepped into a car's path. The car swerved and honked a long constant tone that slowly died out as the lucky person continued into the night. I thought about how that driver would also have to live with the consequences of my decision. No, there was no easy way, short of wishing for a swift illness or perhaps a lone accident that would not leave havoc in its wake for someone else. Wanting to die while being alive seemed worse than death.

I was so sad. I believe people don't die from suicide they die because of sadness. During this prolonged depression, I did lose a lot of weight, but that didn't make me feel better. I couldn't drive anywhere near the university. I tried to come back to see a show there, but found it unbearable. I had given the most productive years of my life to this institution, and now that time was gone and seemed wasted.

I started writing. Yes, I know, this sounds so common for people in this kind of depression to do, but I did it to try to expunge some sense of confusion and pain. I took a journaling course and found it very satisfying. I excoriated the pages of my journal with anger and resentment. I tried to write poetry that usually made me happy, but now sounded sarcastic and mean. My boys once told me during this first year that I looked like Mr. Burns from *The Simpsons* -- hunched and bent.

Maybe it was time to look in the mirror to search for the truth and my part in it. This took more time than I expected. For the truth is that however people talk about character building through adversity, the learning comes from the healing not the hurt. The TRUTH for me was that I did think the way my new supervisor handled her job WAS horrible and vicious, BUT, I had also become defensive and less productive in those last three years. The TRUTH was that I did have a drinking problem which I had worked on since 1989. I was an AA member and had had several relapses. So, I had to face the TRUTH that I did drink inappropriately that evening of the cast party and I had in the past. AA is a program of rigorous honesty that asks its members to be honest with themselves as the only way to really get over on the disease.

So, first, I began writing again. Second, I renewed my membership with AA. And third, I looked at myself honestly. I also joined another group of women that was a spiritually nurturing group which included meditation.

As a result, my life started to take a slow turn toward a new path. The light was beginning to peek through the forest leaves. Now, there was some peace in my mind. After one year of sheer agony, self-loathing, self-pity and fear, I spent *two more years* adding positive people and activities back into my life.

I now volunteer at a horsemanship center for children and adults with various physical and mental challenges. I loved being back in a barn. I grew up with horses but after college, never had the time to return. It is the best! Fresh air, seeing the positive and empowering effects this riding has on the students, and witnessing others whose challenges far outweigh mine.

And, at age 65, I started a little store front theatre company around the corner from my home. I asked the artists I had worked with from the university over the years to join and other local professional artists from the community that I admired throughout my career, and they said YES!! It is now a well-received company.

It has been hard work. My therapist is kind and tells me without doing the WORK, i.e. writing, finding support networks, and giving back to others, I might not have come out of the other side of this depression. Today, I look forward to new adventures and will walk the final leg of the Camino de Santiago in Spain and France next summer to see what that holds. *After a long, cold winter, the sun is finally shining!*

Cathy

Chapter Two

Faith

"All will be well and all will be well
and every kind of thing shall be well."

- Julian of Norwich

The Perfect Gift

It was Christmas time. As usual, I was over scheduled and had misjudged my organizational skills. I had to decorate the house, finish shopping, prepare for activities at church, manage to find numerous babysitters for weekend parties, write the annual Christmas letter for our cards, wrap gifts, not to mention cook a little, and clean the house for my parents' arrival! My mood was as gloomy as the late December afternoon. How had I done it again? I hauled boxes of Christmas decorations from the basement. The living room rug was covered with glitter and strings of twinkle lights with missing bulbs. I launched an attack on the freshly cut tree, hurrying to get it finished.

I opened an unmarked box and discovered our crèche, wrapped in tissue paper. I immediately felt guilty for my surly attitude, but it didn't stop my hurried preparation. After all the pieces were unwrapped and lined up, I found the perfect spot in our front window for the hand-painted ceramic figures. I placed fresh pine and holly around the stable, and nestled votive lights in the branches. The scene looked beautiful. I began to place the shepherds, wise men and animals. I always saved the holy family for last. Glancing at the clock, I knew I was running out of time, dinner needed to be started. I placed Mary and Joseph around the ceramic manger with the baby Jesus perched on the pale golden straw. Complete.

I started to put the tissue back in the box when I realized I missed the angel. I snatched her out of the box and plunked her on the stable roof top. She wobbled for a second and fell to the floor while I watched in horror. The angel broke into several pieces. After a deep breath and a few tears, I gathered up the pieces and decided I could glue her back together. Rummaging through the kitchen junk drawer I found the glue I needed. Placing the pieces on the counter, I got to work. The angel went back together easily. Almost finished with my project, I realized there was a missing piece. The angel was left with a dime-sized hole right where her heart would have been. I frantically searched the living room, but couldn't find the small missing piece.

I placed the glued, but still broken angel in the stable, and sat back on my heels to gauge the damage. It hit me. God had spoken to my heart in a way that I needed. I saw the broken angel as a symbol for all of us. We look pretty good until someone gets close and sees the brokenness, the empty places, the places that hold anger and suffering and fear. Jesus was born to teach us how to fill up those places, not perfectly restore them, but patch them with the love he brought from God. Instead of looking at the angel as imperfect, I decided she was the perfect herald of our humanity, the perfect messenger of the good news. A broken heart isn't an imperfection; it's a necessity if we are going to receive the gospel. All of my frustration and irritation melted away as I pondered her sweet face.

That afternoon happened years ago, and now when I unwrap the crèche, I am reminded who and whose I am. I remember that like the Christmas angel broke in my haste, I am also broken, no matter how good or happy I might look on the outside. Jesus knows my story and he comes over and over again to fill up my sad and frightened places to make me worthy to stand near him and bask in his light. For many years, my favorite piece of scripture has been from Ephesians, "Glory to God whose power working in us can do more than we can ask or imagine." On that winter afternoon long ago, God reminded me of the real meaning of Christmas. I would have missed it in my hurried attempt to get it all done, but God knew just how to speak to my heart. He took what was tarnished in my spirit and renewed it in ways I could never have imagined. The perfect gift.

Sallie Chellis Schisler

Choose Love

My mother died when I was three days old. Because work was hard to find for my father, I was sent to live with my mother's parents. My father did not live with us, but apparently he would come to visit occasionally. He remarried soon after my mother's death and lived with his new family in Hammond, Louisiana. Within a few years, my two half-brothers were born.

I was 5 and still living with my grandmother when she became very ill. She had breast cancer and the medicine she had to take for it made her even sicker. When she died, I went back to live with my father, my new step-mother and my half-brothers.

Their lifestyle was very different from what I was used to as they lived in the country. I was so little, and I was scared out of my mind to go live with them. My step-mother thought I was a threat and she treated me very, very badly. I had only one dress to wear and often went unbathed. One time, a relative found me locked in a closet. Everyone in the family knew of my mistreatment, including my father, but nothing was done about it.

By the time I was 7, I was ready to die.

My grandmother must have taught me to say my prayers, for I did so. I prayed for God to kill me and take me to heaven to live with my mother. As I lay there, a small, quiet voice told me to be calm and not afraid. I was told that I would have a great love one day and that God would always be with me. I felt a great calmness flow over me and I went to sleep unafraid.

My grandmother also must have instilled in me a great sense of self-worth. The love she gave me and the faith in God she led me to helped sustain me throughout my life.

When I was 13, we moved to Texas. Soon after the move, my father and step-mother divorced. She took her sons and moved to New Orleans. I loved my brothers and was devastated that I would never see them again. As luck would have it, one of my brothers and I ended up going to the University of Texas. I was a junior in college and my brother was a freshman. He decided that it was too expensive and was planning to move back to New Orleans.

At one of our college breaks, he wanted me to come home with him for a visit, which meant that I would see my step-mother. I wanted to see my other brother, but you can't imagine the uproar it caused. Everyone that I was close to - my father, my new step-mother, my grandfather, were all about to die because I was going. I went ahead with my plan and as my brother drove my car, we would have to stop every hour to deal with my guilt. After much soul searching and breast beating, I finally saw the answer. It was so clear to me. I had a choice. I could choose to either join in the hate for his mother, or I could choose to love my brothers. To me there was only one choice.

When I went with my brother to his home and saw my step-mother, I felt a great sense of sorrow for what could have been. We did not then or ever talk about what had happened. We did not talk about forgiveness, but she knew just by me being there, that I had put everything from the past behind me. In later years, I visited her mother many times and on one occasion, she apologized for her daughter's behavior.

The decision to embrace a life with my brothers even if it meant she was a part of it, was very healing for me, and I believe it was also very healing for their mother and grandmother. One of the mantras I have tried to live by my whole life is <u>to have love in my heart, not hate</u>.

Anonymous

Having My Doubts

I'm not ashamed to admit it – I don't know what I believe anymore. That may not seem like a big deal to some people, but coming from a background where there was an answer for everything (usually in the Bible), it's a pretty big admission for me. (I won't go so far as to say I was told what to believe about everything, but if ever I had a question, you can bet there was somebody who could answer it for me.)

I'll tell you what I don't believe anymore. I don't believe there's a God up there in the sky watching every little thing you and I do, and moving me around like a pawn to make sure I get to the right place at the right time so that things turn out just so. I don't believe that when I find a good parking space at Wal-Mart it's because God gave it to me, or that when it starts pouring down rain and I have a long way to walk and my hands are full and I can't find my umbrella that God is mad or disappointed or trying to teach me a lesson.

Sometimes, I think, life just happens. And many times, I think, God lets it.

Several years ago there was a Christian song out called "Life is Hard but God is Good." Every Sunday at my church we sing another song, "God is Good All the Time." Well, I know life is hard, but honestly, there have been Sundays when I've found it difficult to sing about God's goodness. Maybe I can get my brain around the idea that God has a "bigger plan" that is so good I can't comprehend it, but come on, "good" in the way I understand it? All the time? I don't know…

Who knows if God intervenes in our little lives? And, if so, how does He decide when and where and how to jump in? Why do we get just what we asked for some of the time and just the opposite at other times? Before you conclude that "I'm just a little black rain cloud," let me tell you what I *think* I know to be true… now.

I'm pretty sure that God is merciful. I think, somehow, God knows and understands when we've had enough. And, I'd like to think that, just when we get to the point that we can't take one more frustrating, discouraging, disheartening blow, maybe, just maybe, God steps in and makes sure we don't have to.

It's hard for me to feel comfortable saying that life has handed me a raw deal. I've never lost my home in a natural disaster, been the victim of a violent crime, or suffered the loss of either of my parents. Still, I have reached what was, for me, rock bottom. After looking forward to being a mother all my life, I finally met the man of my dreams at thirty-four. Just under the wire, I thought – we can still have a few kids before the clock runs out. No such luck. A couple of years of trying the old-fashioned way led to infertility treatments, and, finally a diagnosis of endometriosis. The chances of my conceiving are very slim.

It felt like a cruel joke, I must say. The "whys" were endless. I wept and wailed and gnashed my teeth, begging God to get off his haunches and make something happen. Suddenly he didn't seem so good anymore, and his "bigger plan" was for the birds.

But somehow, I think God was there through all of that, and I think maybe he even understood. And when I was all finished? Yep - still there. Somehow, the right people showed up to help me heal. And somehow, when all was said and done, I ended up with a beautiful baby girl through a fairly painless adoption process.

So, no, I don't know what I believe. I don't even know if the things that seem true to me now are really so. But when I sit in the dark listening to the sweet sounds my little girl makes when she sleeps, I *think* they might be – must be. This is the child I hoped and prayed and waited and cried for, and God had mercy, and now she's here. Life is hard, no doubt about it. Getting here – right where I want to be – was, at times, horribly painful. But I think, in the end, God was – and is – good.

Margaret Wages

A Good Bargain

At one time, my husband and I cared for our child as well as his two children from a previous marriage. Times were tough and we had trouble making ends meet, so I had to go to work full-time. I accepted a job which was very close to home, which was great, but after 18 months I had taken just about as much as I could possibly take from my difficult boss, so I started looking for another job.

My daughter had started kindergarten and was being picked up by her babysitter after school. A few weeks later, my daughter decided to join a Girl Scout Brownie Troop, and I became one of her leaders. I told the babysitter that she would be going to Brownies every Monday and that I would pick her up at school and take her to the meeting.

The week prior to Brownies beginning, I received a call at work 30 minutes after school had let out, telling me that my daughter hadn't been picked up and she was very upset. I had forgotten to tell the sitter when the meetings would begin! Luckily, I only worked four blocks from her school so I got there very quickly. I had a very difficult time keeping myself pulled together until I put her to bed that night. It had upset me knowing how upset she had been. So, after putting her down for the night I let myself breakdown. I prayed to God that He make it possible for me to quit my job so I didn't have to rely on others to take care of my child after school. I told Him that I would do whatever He had in mind for me, if He could make that happen. Have you ever made such a deal with God? Well, I hadn't before that, and I was shocked at how quickly He could make things happen when the timing is right. Just a couple days later our Christian Education Director at church announced that she had to move out of town. Because I had been her assistant at one time, our Rector asked me to take over her position. Within a week everything fell into place. Remembering my deal with God, I accepted the position. I loved that job and held it for more than seven years.

Vicki Daily

Faith of a Child

I was around three years old when I realized that something wasn't right in our home. A couple of days a week I would awaken first (it turned out those were weekends) and go to the kitchen to "make" things. I can remember very well getting the biggest bowl and pouring flour, milk, eggs and whatever else suited my fancy into it. Sometimes I was on a stool, sometimes on the floor, but there was always a huge mess of fun. I never got in trouble for it. I got in trouble for other things, but not what went on during the weekend mornings. When I was much older I realized it was because my parents were hung over and therefore felt guilty thinking of the danger of having a toddler roaming the house alone. I have read such stories where profound tragedy occurred.

When I was around eight, our family was at our log cabin on the river with a babysitter because my parents went there to drink. Thank goodness they thought to hire a sitter because at one point they got into an argument and one of my parents who was holding a gun, threatened to kill the other. There was a lot of yelling and other bad behavior. I was very scared for them, but not for myself.

Throughout the years it continued. It was not daily, but about three to five times a year my sister and I would be whisked off by friends of the family while our parents went on a week-long bender. And again, my worry was for my parents, not me and my sister.

This isn't a story about my parents' addiction so much as a story about how I always felt protected. It is like having a dark hole to be filled with light. When I prayed I felt an immediate calm. When I wasn't praying I still felt safe and protected. Faith? I think so, but from where at such a young age? Faith is a mystery, yet it has continued throughout my 60 some odd years to get me through family issues and all that the world brings with it, and I am thankful for it every day.

Anonymous

Judy's Prayer

Oh Lord, sometimes my delight in my children
is almost too much to be contained.
I would praise you for them, I would rejoice.

These sons are so tall and strong. Often as I despair of them,
complain of them, their achievements thrill me, their values never
cease to surprise me. Their fervor for the underdog, their compassion
and their unexpected consideration
come just when I think they have failed me
and they will do something so generous, so thoughtful,
that I am astonished.

Thank you, God, for these difficult, curious, incredible sons! No, no,
I dare not proclaim this pride in them to others, but to you, who
fashioned them and sent them to me. You, to whom I often cry out in
my distress, surely you must want to hear and share it. I am proud of
these children, Lord. I rejoice in my sons.

Thank you for them.

Judith Pratt Thompson

Victorious Spirit

Each year while growing up my family made the long trip across Texas to visit relatives. My grandmother (Mamaw) became quite dear to me. Although much time passed between seeing each other, she had a great influence on me during those impressionable early years.

Mamaw had lupus, and her condition grew progressively worse over the years. My earliest memories are of her in a wheelchair. Eventually she became confined to her bed. Although her body became more feeble and helpless, her mind remained strong. God's healing power drenched her spirit and overflowed onto those around her. This was my earliest example of true faith, as though a light shone through her that couldn't be dimmed in spite of her pain.

Spending time with Mamaw filled me with joy. Always optimistic, people often came to visit and remarked how good Mamaw made them feel. They meant to cheer her up, but as she told stories and shared her love, they left with a warm glow.

When we visited, Mamaw told me Bible stories or stories about her life, which added to my spiritual development. Her shining example of the victory of her spirit over the ravages of her body taught a lesson much stronger than mere words.

The last year of Mamaw's life we traveled to spend Christmas with her. I had worked for weeks making a nightgown for her and felt proud of my accomplishment. When we arrived, Mamaw was hardly able to talk or eat. I kept thinking she would get better and return to her usual positive self. She said several times, "I want to go home." Although in her own home, she obviously envisioned a home where she could be healed, made whole and free of pain and suffering.

Christmas was rather somber that year. My great expectation had been the thought of giving Mamaw the nightgown I had so painstakingly made. I knew she would understand how much I loved her if I could just give her this special gift. Unfortunately, that was not to be.

My eyes were opened during that time to an awareness of the suffering of others. For the first time, I more fully understood how fragile and uncertain life is, although we can always find comfort in knowing God is with us no matter what happens. I realized that although she never got to wear the gown I made for her with such love, she was robed in the warmth and light of a love that was far beyond what I could ever give her.

Mamaw's lessons were tested and strengthened 20 years later following my diagnosis of lupus. Thinking about Mamaw's physical condition, my first reaction was one of despair, wondering if I could continue to care for my family. But then, that hope and faith I had seen in Mamaw flowed into my mind, filling me with calmness and peace. With assurance I knew I was not alone, and God would sustain me, whatever happened. I still have times of feeling especially bad and start to become depressed. At those times I remember the lesson I have learned and know that God's spirit within me will always be victorious.

Connie Arnold

Are There No Coincidences?

In my life I have had a series of what I consider to be amazing coincidences that have occurred. Of course I am astonished when they happen, but lately, in addition to the amazement, I feel satisfaction because I have begun to accept these coincidences as "messages" or "signs" that I am following the correct path in life. I will provide a few examples:

About 16 years ago my sister and I rode to Chicago with a family friend who was going there to work for a few months. The deal was we would ride with her, stay with my sister's cousin-in-law at her apartment for a few days to see the sites, and then ride the Amtrak train home. The cousin-in-law was a great hostess, and before we left for the train station, she gave me a book to read for the long ride. She said she had just finished it and loved it, and I could just pass it on when I was finished. It was called *Cold Sassy Tree,* by Olive Ann Burns. Later that day, while waiting for the train, I browsed in some shops, and found a biography about Gilda Radnor called *It's Always Something*, and decided to read it first. In the first chapter or so of Gilda's book, she discussed a book she had read and loved, and it was...... *Cold Sassy Tree*! I was totally freaked out, as it was the only book mentioned in the entire biography.

Then, about 14 years ago I was working my first job after college as an audiologist in Beckley, West Virginia. I was working for an ear, nose and throat doctor, and was not particularly thrilled with the job. I had, however, earned enough money to purchase a fancy new sports car (well I thought it was anyway!), which was white. On my usual drive to work, I saw the same model car I was driving parked in a driveway, but it was black. I noticed that the black version of my car looked sleeker than my car. My thought process started wandering then: "Wow, even black cars look skinnier than white cars! It's just like how wearing black clothes makes you look skinner. Wow, I wonder what would be the worst thing you could wear to look fat, probably a white jumpsuit. Wow, if you wore a white jumpsuit to work with gaudy accessories, that might even be enough to get you fired. Yeah! Like a white jumpsuit, with a gold lame belt and gold lame shoes—that would be the ultimate tacky outfit!" Momentarily I arrived at work and greeted my coworkers, including an older woman who had been working in our business office for just a few weeks. My mouth hung open when I saw her outfit: a white jumpsuit, gold lame belt and gold lame shoes. She'd never worn the outfit before.

Roughly 10 years ago I was working at a larger ear, nose and throat office in Huntington, WV. I began seeing a pediatric hearing aid patient who was normally seen at Cincinnati Children's Hospital. However, the family lived in Huntington, and the mother had asked if they could have minor repairs and ear-mold replacements done in our office, closer to home. When they came in, I would chat with the mother while I was working on the child's hearing aids. One day while reviewing the patient's chart, I noticed that the last four digits of their phone number were the same as my home phone number, with only one digit difference in the three digit prefix. I pointed this out to the mother, who was also surprised at the coincidence. Then I jokingly said, "Maybe the lady who calls our house all the time with a wrong number is trying to reach you!!" We had been receiving calls from the same lady at least once or twice a week for months even when we were not home we would see her name on the caller ID. Laughing about the lady who could not seem to get her phone numbers straight, I said "Yes, maybe Mrs. Dalton is trying to reach you!" The mother stopped laughing and said, "THAT IS MY MOM!!!"

Another incident occurred more recently at my current job. One of my coworkers is very vocal and affectionate and calls nearly everyone by a "pet" nickname. She has called me multiple nicknames over the years, one of which is "Kit Kat." One morning, we were having a conversation in which she referred to me as "Kit Kat," and then said, "You know, Kit Kat is a great nickname for you. That is what I'm going to start calling you permanently," and we laughed about it for a while. My first patient of the day arrived about 10 minutes later: a baby named Katherine who was scheduled to have custom earplugs made. She was brought in by her foster mother, who had multiple other children and who was in the process of adopting Katherine. I mentioned the coincidence of my name also being Katheryn, and we began to discuss nicknames for the name. The foster Mom then said, "Her brothers and sisters call her Kit Kat though because she's so sweet."

Finally, when I was VERY pregnant with my first child, I was driving to visit my parents in a city about forty-five minutes away. It was a beautiful day and I had this thought, "Wow, it is so beautiful today. It's almost too beautiful, like it can't be this perfect. I think I'm going to see a car accident." I kind of had a feeling of dread, and would you believe, not two miles later, I saw a Honda Passport rolling in the median, with stuff flying out of the car windows. I pulled over and called 911, but since several other people had already stopped to help, I didn't get out. Also, I was nine months pregnant, and I think the stress of what I saw was giving me early contractions.

Coincidence? Fate? Divine intervention? None of these stories I relate were earth shattering, life-saving or anything more than mere coincidence, or were they? I like to think they serve as messages to let me know my life is on the right path, and I welcome them now, even if they render me agog.

Katheryn Seymour Monk

Looking Up

To my friends:

I was raised a minister's child, but I was blessed/cursed with an overactive brain and a very passionate heart. Many times in my life I veered from the righteous path I was raised to follow. The last few years have been painful and difficult for many reasons, but mostly, I have discovered, because I was not looking up. My father, a healthy and fit 66, recently became very ill. Over the couple of months it has taken to discover the nature of his illness, I looked up and I was

> *The biopsy results confirm the initial diagnosis of idiopathic pulmonary fibrosis, the lung disease that causes slow suffocation as the lungs lose their ability to transfer oxygen. The final diagnosis was made by the Mayo Clinic in Phoenix. They are the recognized experts in these interstitial lung diseases. My pulmonary doctor is starting me on high-dose Prednisone for 3 months. If that doesn't kill me, then I'm not sure what Plan B will be yet. I have an appointment with the pulmonary doctor on the 31st. There is no cure; only the hope that drug treatment can slow down the progress of the disease. The data says it helps about 30% of patients.*
>
> *I have a choice. I can curl up and play dead until I die, or I can try to do the best that I can with what I have left. I choose to keep trying. My health situation has created a greater sense of urgency for me. It provides clearer focus, and emphasis on what is really most important. It clears up fuzziness. That's a good thing.*

shown a path that would lead me home. Once I chose to follow that path, God cleared all obstacles and made it relatively easy for me to make the journey I needed to make. I am going home to be with my family. I will lose my father soon. I am so glad God rattled my cage before it was too late.

Above is an email I received from my father today (you'll note the "Patricia"-style dry humor. Yes, I am my father's daughter - and very proud of it!):

The moral to this story: LIVE today and LOVE with all your heart. Now!

I am proud that my father has chosen to live while he still has life. I hope that when it is my time to make that same choice, I have his strength and courage.

If I sent you this note, it is because you are especially important to me, and I wanted to share this story with you because you are my friends. I know I am hard to know, but the up side is that the few friends I have get a bigger chunk of my heart than they would get if I collected friends willy-nilly. If I have been remiss in communicating this before now, I love you and I thank you for being you. Each of you has touched me in profound and significant ways and has made my life better for having known you. Thank you for that. I hope I did something good for you, too. If not, well, here's a little something: Please don't wait to live your lives. Live life every single day. Find beauty in small things. And if you're on a dark path, know that there are other paths to choose. It really is that simple.
Much love,

Patricia Wells

Against The Odds

Having had a miscarriage at 12 weeks and then a D&C (dilation and curettage), I miraculously got pregnant again straight away, despite it having taken us six months to get pregnant the first time. After four or five weeks I began having severe pain on my side and was referred to the early pregnancy unit. They couldn't see anything to signify a pregnancy, but they also couldn't see anything sinister, as one-sided pain was often the first sign of an ectopic pregnancy. So, they took my blood to establish if I was pregnant and recommended another scan and blood test in 48 hours to establish if this pregnancy was viable.

The blood test confirmed that I was pregnant.

I returned as requested and though the scan still showed nothing and the blood test showed my hormone levels had risen, it seemed it could not sufficiently show a viable pregnancy. If my hormone levels goes down, the pregnancy is being lost, because it should double every other day for a healthy pregnancy. If it increases but not that much it means its implanted, but not in the right place. The suspicion was that I had an ectopic pregnancy.

We had to return another three times at 48-hour intervals to have another scan and blood test each time to see if anything could be identified in the womb or otherwise, and to track my hormone level. There continued to be nothing on a scan and my HCG continued to rise....very, very slowly. This is the gold test for an ectopic and we were told it was 99.9% an ectopic pregnancy and that I would have to take an anti-cancer drug to destroy the misplaced implantation.

We got two second opinions who both said the same thing. By this point, nearly 10 days had passed. We went for a final HCG test and scan along with a progesterone test as the final 0.01% - it was expected to be low. We got the progesterone test result - it was 60! We had expected it to be under 20!

We had to wait overnight to speak to the doctor and went for the final scan and hormone level check. During my scan the doctor could tell immediately there was something in the womb and he announced that suddenly my hormone level had doubled since the last test and upon further analysis the 'thing' in my womb looked like a totally normal pregnancy. My baby was the 0.01%!

One thing that will always stand out to me is the doctor saying, "It doesn't matter how far science comes, it can't second guess nature. It's a remarkable thing." It was actually a huge struggle having had to get our heads around the fact we *weren't* having a baby, and to then be told that we *were*. Naturally, we were super nervous through the whole pregnancy, but as the doctor implied…nature prevailed.

And now, we have Hugo.

Rebecca Jenkins

The People

The people shouted at them
let us come in
they glowered back
you may not enter
we know what is best for you.

He had stood in that place
beloved - denied
and the people shouted
crucify Him
because they were afraid.

After the confrontation
the authorities asked
what do you want
one by one the people answered
peace

Suzanne Baker

(Written during our trip to Jerusalem, Easter 2010. The Israeli
authorities would not let us into the Holy Sepulcher to see Holy Fire
on Easter Saturday. In the context of the present fighting in
Jerusalem between Israelis and Palestinians, they polled ordinary
citizens on both sides about what they want to happen.)

Never Alone

I am a singer in a rock 'n roll band. Probably not one you've ever heard of – we're just a small group at St. Paul's Catholic Church in Westerville, Ohio. Yes, we are a Christian rock 'n roll band called *Still Standing*. No, we're not named after the Elton John song but because, no matter what we have faced or what we're going through in this life, we still believe very much in God and we're still here! We all have our stories and we all know it is by the grace of God that we are still standing.

We sing a variety of Christian tunes and a few Roman Catholic ones thrown in for good measure. One of my favorites is the song *Never Alone* by Barlow Girl. The song talks about how, even though we might not be able to see or hear God when we need Him most, we have faith that He is always there. I sing the opening of this song as a solo. It's a hard song to sing, so I have to get to a place where I can really tell the story convincingly. So I go to the place where I could not feel, hear or see God and yet I knew He was there anyway. The place is the doorway to the operating room where I had my second ectopic surgery.

Right before I sing that song, I close my eyes and I am lying on a gurney being wheeled into surgery. I have huge butterflies in my stomach (even with the pre-pain-meds). I'm looking right at my doctor, Patricia Teach, M.D.-extraordinaire (no joke – my ectopic exploded on me in her waiting room. As the paramedics were loading me into the rig, out came Dr. Teach in her coat. I asked her where she was going. She said, "I'm going to follow you to the hospital – I'll be right behind you." And that is why she is my doctor now and forever, amen.) I see her face with her mask down around her chin. She smiles at me and tells me it's all going to be all right. I lost a lot of blood when the ectopic blew. I had to have a full pint of blood during surgery.
They ended up having to do a cesarean section incision and took out my last fallopian tube. The babies were twins nestled together. The surgery was successful and I'm alive.

So, when I reach the chorus: "I cried out with no reply and I can't feel you by my side. So, I'll hold tight to what I know – you're here and I'm never alone," I think, "Thank you God, for the miracle of life, however you choose to give it."

Peggy Bourke McCort

***

Psalm 40

I waited patiently for the Lord; He stooped to me and heard my cry.
He lifted me out of the desolate pit, out of the mire and clay;
He set my feet upon a high cliff and made my footing sure.
He put a new song in my mouth, a song of praise to our God; *
many shall see, and stand in awe, and put their trust in the Lord! *

From the *Book of Common Prayer*

Chapter Three

Girl Power

"I am not afraid. I was born for this!"

- Joan of Arc

Will You Let Me Be Your Servant?

The first time I was admitted to the hospital, I was in my 50s. I was a working woman, loved my job, felt successful and productive, and most importantly, my spiritual life was abloom. My husband and I met with the pastors of our church every Tuesday morning at 7:00 to pray for the church, those in need, and the pastors themselves.

I was diagnosed with a chronic disease and could not seem to stabilize. After 18 days, I was released to go home with Home Health coming by often to check on me for about three months. I felt close to death during that time and one of the conversations I had with my pastor made me realize how weak my faith was. I told him, "I didn't plan on being sick so young," and Pastor Ron replied, "It is not your plan. It is His."

Now in my 60s after the third visit to the hospital, I am recovering from a related problem associated with the chronic disease. After four years of many doctors in a large metropolitan city trying to reach a diagnosis, the answer was found after we moved to a small town in West Virginia. The confusion I had been experiencing was not as we thought - a combination of two pharmaceuticals that shouldn't be taken together - but was actually too much ammonia in my blood which is sometimes caused by the chronic disease. I have crossed a major threshold with this new information and plan of attack!

When I left the hospital after a week, I thought back over that time about how frightened I was. I was also thankful that the Lord once again blessed me with a way to handle a very restricted diet and with a way to serve Him. During my stay, two members of patients' families approached me, asked if I was a Christian and that I pray for their family member. I happened to be on the oncology floor and it was not unusual for that floor to be the last earthly home for a patient. That was so healing to be able to comfort someone else. I realized the Lord gave me renewed clarity of mind and a purpose. He was there all the time waiting on me to lean on Him; to take my eyes off myself and to love others.

Dear Heavenly Father, you have numbered the stars in the sky and the grains of sand in the ocean. You know each one of us completely in the worst of our fear and rage and quiet desperation, and also in the best of times. Thank you for loving me, for teaching me, and leading me. Thank you for my family who tried to help me during my time of confusion. Help me be a blessing to each one of them. In Jesus' name I pray. Amen.

Susan Hargis Hash

A Father's Love

I have many memories of when I was a child. Some are very good, some not so good. It is funny how certain events in your life stay with you forever and others are quickly forgotten. I was three years old when I was having trouble with my legs. They didn't seem to want to straighten out and have me walk normally. It is hard for a three year old to tell her parents exactly what is wrong. My parents just knew that I was having a lot of difficulty walking with my swollen legs. This was over fifty years ago when juvenile rheumatoid arthritis (JRA) was not very well known. I can remember going from doctor to doctor trying to determine what the problem was. I look back at how very strong and brave my parents were dealing with their toddler having a crippling disease at such a young age. I, not knowing any better and thinking the world was a wonderful place, didn't have any fears of not walking or being "normal." I just knew my parents loved me and would fix whatever was causing the pain and discomfort. Being a parent and grandparent myself, I realize now how very scared and troubled Mom and Dad were. It is one thing to deal with a disability for an adult or yourself. It is very difficult to deal with a child having the pain, discomfort and disfigurement that sometimes come with JRA. I was not aware of my diagnosis. Even though the doctors had told my parents that I would never walk again, it was unknown to me. So, I just assumed that this was a little problem that would eventually go away as I got bigger. There was no question in my mind that I would grow up relatively normal. I remember not understanding why my mom and dad were so upset because I knew everything was going to be just fine. This is what my mind, body, and heart told me even at this very young age.

After surgery on one knee and having treatments for my condition, I ended up staying at Duke Hospital in Durham, North Carolina for many weeks. In a way, it seems like yesterday that my dad took me up to North Carolina. Mother stayed in Gainesville, Florida to take care of my older sister. The one thing I remember about the hospital stay is that my dad could not stand to see me in a wheelchair, so he brought a little red wagon up to the hospital to pull me around. The nurses thought this was a great idea so the children wouldn't feel like they were really sick but that they were just having a ride in a red wagon. The hospital didn't look so scary anymore. We know that most hospitals now use wagons instead of wheelchairs whenever possible. I had no idea how much my father was ahead of his time in handling my situation.

My story ends very well. I did walk, run, play and became very normal (some of my family and friends may think differently). I never thought negatively about any situation. There were very sad times, but I choose to remember the very happy times. I believe the positive responses and encouragement I received from my parents have carried me through life, knowing that nothing is stronger than your own self being and faith. I am grateful to my mom and dad for teaching me one of life's lessons. I just hope I can pass on the positive, loving attitude that I received. I am a firm believer in thinking the best in not the best of circumstances.

Barbara Byelick

If the Shoe Fits

I had never been to Las Vegas, so when the opportunity to go came up because of a business trip for my husband, I took it.

We were there for a weekend and once while he was in a meeting I went shopping. I was looking around one shop when I came across a beautiful dress. I might not have given it a second thought had I not just lost some weight, but I tried it on and loved it! The saleswomen were so encouraging. I had them take a picture of me in the dress because I wasn't sure my husband would let me get it. There was a comma in the price tag and I normally am a "Maxxinista" if you catch my meaning. Lucky for me, they were having a sales event where if your purchase was over $1,000, you could get $300 in merchandise free. So, I found some shoes to go with it that were to die for. Again, not normally my style, but I was in Vegas, baby!

At lunch I showed my husband the photo of me in the dress and he thought I looked great. However, the price tag was, in a word, insane. Back I went to the store later that day...not to buy the dress, of course, but to buy the shoes as a consolation prize. They weren't cheap either, but I had to have them, even if I couldn't have the dress.

That night, when my husband saw the shoes he thought I had lost my mind. Hadn't we talked about how expensive they were? Yes. But in my defense, I thought he said no to the dress, not the shoes. So, knowing he was upset about the big spending I, ahem, "apologized" as only a wife on a weekend trip with her husband knows how...wearing the shoes and little else.

Fast forward to a New Year's Eve party with several of our closest friends. It was the end of the night and having been over-served I regaled the women who were gathered in the kitchen of my shoes escapade. They loved it! It was funny, I'll have to admit, but I wasn't counting on someone sharing the story with the men. I was mortified! Humiliated! What would they think of me?

I couldn't bear to wear the shoes again, knowing that our friends would know what had happened. Into my closet they went. Then, one day, a girlfriend mentioned going away on a trip with her husband for their anniversary. Figuring the only way out of my humiliation was to have my friends and their husbands make their own memories, I took down the box of shoes, tied it up in a bow and delivered them to my friend to borrow for the weekend, wishing her all the best. Then another friend borrowed them for a cruise. Another borrowed them for a wedding. And so on, and so on, and so on. They've been to The Greenbrier Resort, The Homestead, California, and New York City for romantic trips, a wedding, a class reunion, etc.

I am thrilled they are getting worn and happy that my friends have been a part of this sisterhood of the traveling shoes. Everyone needs a little Vegas in their life, right?

Elizabeth Castle

Whistling Girl

My oldest daughter, Kate, wanted to learn how to whistle in the worst way. She was only a first grader at the time. She pursed her lips, she blew, she spit a bit, too, all to no avail, and so she was getting frustrated that she couldn't master this seemingly simple human body trick. She didn't give up though, and one day, the magic happened. She pursed, she blew and a reedy little sound came forth – much to her wondrous surprise! She was tickled with herself – pure and simple. And then she didn't stop whistling. So she whistled all the time – everywhere we went. Mindless birdlike sounds, chirps and tweets and trailing twittering, though she did try a few simple nursery rhyme tunes here and there.

At first I didn't mind it so much. Make a joyful noise, I thought. Whistle on, girl. But I started to go a little batty because of it, especially when her younger sister, Rebecca – always the imitator – tried to follow suit without any luck. I know where she gets this whistling business. I only have to look in the mirror – she is my miniature self. I was the same way when I was a little girl, always whistling a little something as I went on my merry way. One of my fondest childhood memories involves whistling and skipping. I was about 8, I guess, and with my great-grandmother, Anna Lee McLean Ewing. We were walking up the sidewalk from her house to the restaurant she owned and operated, The Sandhills Café, located on the corner of the center crossroads of our small town of Candor, North Carolina. I was skipping alongside her, making circles around her, just whistling away, being a general pest. Nanny, as she was known to family, and Miz Ewing as she was known by everybody else far and wide, was a frail looking, birdlike woman with a steel constitution. I can picture us now – what a pair!

"A whistling girl and a crowing hen, never come to a good end," she called out to me in her own thin, chirpy voice. I stopped, wrinkled up my forehead in a frown, and gave her a look only an 8-year-old can produce. "What does that mean?" I responded. Nanny just looked back at me and emitted this mischievous little laugh that she had; her blue eyes twinkled behind her wire eye glass frames. She grabbed my hand and said, "It means stop whistling."

I skipped on ahead, puzzled, but undeterred. I whistled on.

Over the years I pondered her words. It became one of my favorite sayings, but it wasn't until I was much older that I understood what it really meant – that whistling was considered an improper thing for a girl or woman to do, and she was better off being seen and not heard. Nanny was born in 1903 and was raised through The Great Depression, a defining era for a generation who learned how to do a lot with too little. She was a pioneer of her time – a businesswoman who owned and operated her own restaurant and hotel – a whistling girl in her own right and she passed it on.

I caught myself whistling the other day. It was a gorgeous, early fall afternoon, and I felt good enough to be skipping down the street, though I didn't. The memory of that day and that 8-year-old girl came rushing back to me, making me wistful for more of that youthful courage I used to unfurl at the world. I determined to dig a little deeper for the courage to step outside my comfort zone because it's important that my girls don't lose sight of the fact that they are the progeny of a long line of strong women who found a way to whistle. My girls will only know that if I embody what Nanny had to teach. So whistle on, my chicks, whistle on.

Bonnie Davis

We've Still Got It

For the past three summers, a group of friends and I have gathered for a Girls Weekend complete with spa treatment, shopping, eating, talking, and lots of laughing. Between the six of us there are 13 children. We have a great time together and I always find myself inspired when the weekend is over.

This time there were only four of us as we took on a quaint, little town in the mountains of North Carolina. We are a cute bunch. After having all these kids we are in decent shape. We allow for some retail therapy that doesn't include the "Circo" brand, and have come out of the fog of sleep deprivation enough to know what current events are swirling around in the news. Hip? You bet. Hot? Mmm, we're not feelin' it. Or are we?

A couple of events made me wonder…

The first instance occurred as we left the spa after much pampering and relaxation. As we're heading to the car an older man noticed us, smiled and, I think in an attempt to chat us up, asked, "You girls from around here?" I'm thinking, "Sir. It's not going to happen." A couple of girls answered him and then he proceeded to ask us where we're going for dinner that night. Bless his heart, I think he was just excited and started talking to us before his brain caught up with him.

The second and more direct occurrence happened when we met up with another friend at a local watering hole after dinner. It was a nice place with a diverse crowd. And by diverse, I mean the ages of the patrons varied between college kids to Granny & Gramps. (Perhaps we would meet our parking lot suitor after all…) I digress.

At one point our friend leaves and we are left sitting at a large banquette area. Not for long. Before we could start talking about how tired we were, that our feet hurt and we just wanted to go to sleep along came a young man. He looked to be 12 and noticing the chairs available, sat himself and his buds at our table. He had his swagger on for sure. Having reached his alcohol limit and then some, it did not stop him from working this lovely group of women. When he finally got around to telling us his name, which was Cody, one friend could barely hold in her laughter and all she could muster was, "Of course it is."

I said to him, "Cody, I can't help but notice we don't have any drinks." Never had I ever been so brazen, but I thought someone should help this boy with his manners. On point, the Codster whipped out his dad's credit card and sent one of his homies to get some beers. Our treat? A dark, thick pilsner that was probably the draft on special that night. Sigh. Boys, boys, boys.

A couple of his cronies chimed in. One who was sitting next to me was a long-haired surfer type who was quite possibly named Justin. Justin is telling his college woes of changing his major a few times and being upset that he still has to pay for the classes he already took even though he's not in that major anymore. He's thinking about grad school in Miami. I told him I knew someone who had gone there and studied architecture. (I left out that it was my husband of 13 years.) "Cool," says Justin.

Trying other tricks to impress us, the boys throw in that Cody is a twin. His brother, who we'll call, well, Zach, is sitting at the end of the table. Not quite as far gone as Cody, Zach sits in his ball cap and nods. Wow, twins! This is where my friend could have inserted that she has 7-year-old twins – small world – but she refrained.

We did discuss our jobs. Kind of. Rather than go down the line and say "I'm a stay-at-home mom and work part-time", we reverted back to our former jobs of distinction to relay that we were in marketing, public policy, education, and public relations. We were able to skirt the topic because lo and behold, Cody had fallen asleep, his head leaning back against a picture hanging on the wall. Not to let this go unnoticed his friends grabbed some drink stirrers from the bar and promptly put them up his nose and in his mouth. Hilarity ensued. I felt this was a Kodak moment and scooted over to have one of the girls take a picture of us. Oh. My. Gosh. The co-eds saw my friend's camera and wha-bam! Out came the iPhones and what not and there were flashes everywhere. Keenly aware that momentarily I might end up on Facebook or YouTube, I thought this was a perfect time to call it a night. So, we said good-bye to those crazy college kids and headed home.

After telling my sister this story, she told me that young guys are totally into older women. That yes, they might have been drinking, but it wasn't a beer goggles situation. They were probably genuinely interested in us. And, when asked how old they thought we were, one answered, "Twenty-two at least." Oh, at least, my visually-impaired friend, at least.

Elizabeth Hash Lopina

– – –

An Extended Family

I was 5 years old, sitting in an oversized dining room chair. My feet dangled miles above the floor. "Why are we sitting in the dining room?" I inquired. "Because Daddy and I have something to talk to you about." *I'm in trouble* I thought. *They know I peed outside*. I quickly tried to conjure up the best possible excuse for public urination. Efficiency! It sounded reasonable and it would appeal to their pragmatism. I would simply explain that I was in the yard and it was quicker to pee outside than inside. But before I could rationalize my behavior, my Mom dropped a bomb. "You were adopted," she said. I didn't fully grasp the meaning of those words at the time, but they would have a profound impact on my life from that point forward.

I began to cry. I was not angry. I was not sad. I felt isolated. I looked different, acted different, and had different genetics than my Mom, my Dad, and my brother. Then I decided that I loved my family, I liked my room, and I had great toys. So it was settled, I would stay. I was happy once again; however, questions about my identity and original family haunted me for the next two decades. Who were my biological parents? Did I look like them? Did I act like them? Who was I like? The answers would come 20 years later when I hired a private investigator to locate my birthmother.

In May 2000, I met my birthmother outside of the dentist's office where she worked. It was a surreal experience to observe our physical similarities. Once we stopped inspecting each other, we drove to her home. She answered all of my questions and provided me with pictures of herself and her family. She told me her life story and I quickly realized how dissimilar we were. So, I sought to find someone more similar to me and contacted my biological father. Although I never expected to develop a relationship with him, a special connection quickly formed. My biological father and I share many personality traits, a similar outlook on life, and we seem to know what the other is thinking without even saying a word. I do not look exactly like him. I don't always act like him and our interests are not always the same, yet we have a marvelous relationship.

I would like to meet some of my other biological relatives, however, I am no longer seeking people who are just like me. I am my own person, and I think it's best that way.

Annemarie Wasilauskas Lopina

Chapter Four

Learning

"We live in deeds not years
In thoughts not breaths
In feelings not figures on a dial
We should count time by heart throbs
He most lives who thinks most, feels noblest, acts the best."

— Philip James Bailey, *Festus: A Poem*

What Will People Say?

Sometimes neither age, nor experience, nor common sense can give the correct answer to a situation. The following is a case in point:

One of my mother's favorite sayings was, "What will people say?" Living in a small town where everyone knew-and discussed-everyone else's business, I realized that hers was not merely a rhetorical question. My sister and I grew up knowing well what was expected of us and knowing that our parents, grandparents, and all the neighbors were watching and reporting. We heeded the rules.

Then came the next generation-my children. Suddenly I was the mother of a teenage daughter who seemed totally oblivious to "what will people say" and likewise oblivious to "mother knows best." "Perhaps this is the way teenagers behave in this generation," her father and I said. "Or maybe we have somehow failed as parents." With each dramatic incident, we parents dared to hope: "This will be the last problem. She's maturing. She's in college now."

When the announcement of her pregnancy came, we were devastated. I suggested abortion, adoption-everything but leaving the country. True, I was concerned about "what will people say," but even more concerned about a young woman (she was 21) who had dropped out of college and who did not seem at all ready for motherhood. When she insisted that she wanted to keep the child, I made it clear that I would not be responsible if she changed her mind. Her father and I grieved. We fretted. We worried, but we did not break our relationship. We were very concerned for her health and that of her child.

To show her independence and resolve, she got an apartment, a part time job, and gave birth to a healthy baby boy. When I suggested that she and the baby come to our home from the hospital, she declined. She went home to her apartment and managed quite well with occasional help and good daycare. In the following three years, our single-mom daughter returned to college, made excellent grades, graduated with two degrees (a B.S. and an M.S. in English and

Special Education) all while taking care of her son. She has been a wonderful, caring mother and vows that this child saved her life by giving her purpose and direction.

And what about the doubting mother (now grandmother)? Obviously mother did NOT know best in this situation. That child has been and is the joy of my life. I love him dearly and have enjoyed every minute of his life. Our family is very proud of him and his mother and all they have accomplished. As to "what will people say," I am glad our daughter was not concerned in this particular case. She followed her heart. Or was it intuition? Or perhaps God? If she had listened to me or worried about "what will people say," it would have been a huge mistake for her, for our family, and for everyone who knows our very special grandson.

Sue Addington

Faith, Hope and Love

In 1979, I was married and my husband, who was a physician, and I had two sons. I was also helping to raise my half-brother. I was 39 years old and I had a stroke. It left a large blood clot in the center of my brain. The doctors were able to see the clot with the hospital's new cat-scan equipment that had just been installed three weeks before my stroke. (Ironically, my husband was partly responsible for getting it here.) I was operated on and the clot was removed, along with much of the center of my brain which involved my speech and balance.

After a very long and scary hospital stay I went home. This was very difficult for the children who were 7, 11, and 18. I could not walk, speak clearly or do anything I had done before. Whereas before I was healthy and active, now I had to learn to rely on others for help for nearly everything. Learning to trust people to care for me was an important life lesson.

There were no home physical therapy services at the time. I had to set up and do everything at home. Recovery was very slow. It has been more than 32 years ago and my therapy is still going on today. Walking is still very difficult and at times people who don't know me think I am drunk. I have had to create new and additional activities to remain active. I can do none of the things I used to do before such as swimming in the ocean, playing tennis, riding a bike, playing the piano, or running. However, I can cook, think, type, write, talk, and, most important of all, love.

This was definitely a near-death experience for me and when I hear people blame God for bad things that happen, saying it's His will or something just as stupid, I say "NO!" Many tragic things happen in life and God will give you the strength to help you fight through it. His love for us is beyond our understanding, but it has sustained me throughout my life.

Marianne Bell Tweel

Perspective

After many years of not being a part of a Sunday school class or Bible study, I came across a group that fit well into my life. The group consisted of women of varying ages. In my mid-30s, I was on the younger end of the spectrum. I really enjoyed the women in the group and considered myself lucky to have befriended these older, wiser women.

One particular day we were discussing the idea of doing for others. There were about a dozen women in class that day so I ended up sitting behind a few of them. At some point, I felt comfortable enough to raise my hand and share a story about how one of my neighbors had generously offered to watch my kids so I could do something for myself. Then the next week I returned the favor for her. It was kind of an "it takes a village" example in my life. I had started the story by saying something like, "You know I'm struggling with things right now, I mean, we're all struggling…" (I was referring to our community's recent loss of jobs and the economic downturn) and proceeded to tell my story. A few minutes after I shared, I realized how stupid I was to say what I said, for in front of me sat a woman who was new to our church. She was a refugee from Ghana and had moved to our city with her husband and three daughters, having had to leave children behind in a refugee camp. She and her family were living in cramped housing until they could get on their feet. She also had breast cancer and was undergoing chemotherapy.

I felt like an idiot. I was so embarrassed that I had voiced my problems to the class. Nobody said anything to me about it, but I will never forget that feeling I had. Yes, my family was struggling financially and things were pretty grim, but I was healthy, my children were healthy and safe, we had a home, and we had food. Now, whenever I start to feel sorry for myself and my situation, I think of her and others who have to shoulder a much bigger burden than I.

Anonymous

Sticks and Stones

Living in the United States, my mixed heritage has been all of the following: interesting, fulfilling, and fun…heartbreaking, difficult and embarrassing. Now an adult and having been through many of life's lessons, I completely embrace my uniqueness and know my mixed heritage has a lot to teach me and others.

Growing up in the Midwest and being half American (Scottish-Welsh decent) and half Japanese, I experienced prejudice and discrimination from grade school through college, and sadly still see it today. When I was young, it mainly involved name-calling or making fun of my physical appearance like my eyes, my face, etc. that bothered me. Sometimes it was behind my back. Sometimes it was right in my face. Kids would make fun of my mother, too, which really hurt. It was cruel, but she always handled it gracefully, and fortunately, sometimes didn't seem to notice or understand when it was happening.

I can remember in grade school, a few times I was hit or kicked by kids, mainly by boys. I can only attribute this to it being a period of time (the '70s & '80s) when people were not as sensitive to diversity and didn't know any better. But then again, they could have just been mean-spirited little children. I remember bringing yummy sheets of seaweed to 5th grade Show & Tell. Most of the kids liked the taste until I told them what it was and they spit it out.

My sister and I were only two of a very small group of Asian children in the Dayton/Mason, OH schools. There were times that I could tell girls were jealous of me and they tried to physically fight me. They would claim it was over a guy, or some other silly thing, but I knew it was because they were insecure and because I was different from them. I represented something they didn't understand or accept.

When I was in junior high I didn't always handle being Asian-American well. At the mall or grocery store I would walk well in front of my Mom so people didn't think I was with her. And, though she was always graceful and nice to people anywhere we went, I often tried to distance myself from her. There were times, however, that I had to defend her in stores when the cashier or someone in the store was rude to her because she was "a foreigner." They were not expecting me to defend her, and it shut most of them up.

In her defense, my mother was always nice to everyone, but if someone upset me or picked on me she was a Mama Bear and would handle the situation. Sometimes that meant calling other parents or the school. And if she got mad, look out! Yoshi was hell on wheels! It was the only time she raised her voice to other people.

I could talk to my sister about my problems, or friends who saw it happening, but my sister actually had it a lot worse than I did. Where I would defend myself or just get through it, my sister would keep a lot of her hurt feelings bottled up inside. She was quiet and shy and had only a few friends. She was picked on mercilessly some days. Sometimes it got so bad that she contemplated suicide.

Enduring adversity made us much stronger and able to have sympathy and compassion for others. I do not like bullies, obviously, and will not tolerate that kind of behavior now as an adult. I speak up when I see it or experience it, if needed, whether it's for me or someone else. I wouldn't care as much, except that there have been children present who see and hear some of the behavior, and I believe prejudice is learned and taught by families.

Years ago, I worked for a Japanese company with both American and Japanese men. The Japanese men were very hard-working, but could be stubborn and chauvinistic. I had to tell some of them the same thing two to three times before they'd listen and acknowledge that my information was correct. The younger ones did not act that way to me though and seemed to respect me for the independent American woman that I am. They would tell me that I was more Japanese than some of the girls in Japan in my mannerisms and behavior. I knew it was my mother's influence.

Looking back on my years growing up, I am ashamed of my behavior, but I did it because I was tired of being picked on, getting so many dirty looks and having people be rude. Now, I am very proud of my heritage and have been for years. Between meeting relatives over the years, traveling to Japan as a child and positive influences from our Japanese family friends, I continue to strive to appreciate the beauty of this ancient culture. I have tried to learn more about Japan and the people, as well as how to speak the language. I have become involved with the Japan American Society through social events and volunteering, and I truly enjoy it.

Once, an American boss asked me how it felt to be between two worlds, to see two different viewpoints, yet not feeling as though I fully belonged to either one. I told him I just tried to do my best.

Being multi-cultural has made my life interesting, and I enjoy having two vastly different frames of reference and embrace them both. I am proud of my mother and the Japanese heritage she has passed on to me. I am no longer ashamed or embarrassed to be looked at differently.

Being a "half-breed" wasn't always a walk in the park. The jeers and bullying hurt me and my family, but now I can say with confidence that I am who I am because of all of it. I am proud of who I am.

私は平和午前

Christine Akiko (Autumn) Lucas

Her New Friend

My sister and I were close when we were kids. She was younger than me and I loved playing with her hair, being silly, watching cartoons, and playing dress-up. We were close like sisters should be until one day when she found a new friend. By this time, I did not live at home anymore. When I would come back to visit she was rarely around, and when she was around, she wasn't always engaged in what was going on. She would rather be spending time with her new friend.

Friends are supposed to be nice to you and support you, but this friend didn't seem to do that. This friend often made my sister feel bad about herself, which led to poor decisions and a lot of mistakes she wouldn't have made before they met. Her behavior towards our parents also declined. This friend was such a bad influence she often made my sister lie, take advantage and basically have a lack of respect for those who did the most for her. With a friend who was always taking instead of giving, this relationship seemed to be very one-sided. I know my sister made her own choices, but it was like she was under a spell where this new friend was concerned.

Life went on. We all got together for family visits, but for so long my sister and I didn't really connect. Where I was envious of her lack of rules, lack of retribution and assumed freedom, she didn't seem to care much about me and kept herself at a distance.

This friend had put a wedge between us and between her and our parents. It affected the whole family. Excuses were made for her behavior. Leeway was given. Failures and mistakes were swept under the rug. This new friend really had everyone snowed.

Years went by without change until one day when my sister's friend got her in really big trouble. Her friend led her to have all of this "fun," but then turned on her and left her hurt and alone.

And yet, that is when things started to turn around for my sister.

Her family came to her rescue and she never saw that friend again. She reached out to the one more powerful than herself, and still prays to him every day, "God, grant me the serenity to accept the things I cannot change. The courage to change the things I can. And the wisdom to know the difference."

If you guessed her "friend" was substance abuse, you would be right. It is a disease. She was under its spell. But, through hard work, dedication and the help of many wonderful friends who are fighting the same fight, she has gotten healthy and gotten sober…seven years and counting.

As for our relationship, we are closer than ever before. Amends have been made and we have open discussions about the past, the present and the future. We share stories about each other that happened years ago that neither of us knew about. We talk on the phone for hours, share our ups and downs, trade parenting stories and tips, and laugh until we cry. I am beyond thrilled to have my sister back.

Anonymous

"Each one of us here today will at one time in our lives look upon a loved one who is in need and ask the same question: We are willing to help, Lord, but what, if anything, is needed? For it is true we can seldom help those closest to us. Either we don't know what part of ourselves to give or, more often than not, the part we have to give is not wanted. And so it is those we live with and should know who elude us. But we can still love them - we can love completely without complete understanding."

- Norman Maclean, *A River Runs Through It*

Finding Mothers

Our mothers are our biggest fans and strongest supporters. They stand by us when others will not. They believe in the innate goodness of our hearts even when we are at our worst. Their faith in our abilities usually exceeds our own. The world is full of examples of mothers laying down their lives for their children or giving up everything they have to be sure their children are safe, fed and protected. We don't think there is anything that we can do to make our mothers turn away from us. Except sometimes, there is. Sometimes, there is a poison that finds its way in to a mother's heart and causes it to tell her daughter, "We had your first 37 years; they can have the next 37."

That was the email I received from my mother two days after hurricane Katrina ravaged the gulf coast of America, where families were left homeless, torn apart and frightened. She easily shunned me. Her only child.

The circumstances by which my mother opted out of my life could fill three seasons of Dr. Phil. My story isn't about the why of it; it's about the survival of it.

The days following that e-mail and the horrible phone conversations that accompanied it (I live five states away from my parents) were some of the darkest of my life. Not only was I trying to cope with the issue of their anger about my relationship with my biological father, but I was learning that my mother's love was *not* unconditional. I couldn't quite grasp the latter. I am a mother. My son had just turned 4 and the thought of dismissing him from my life because he betrayed me somehow was...*and is*.... simply impossible to imagine.

But life goes on and there is work to do, so we find ways to survive when our heart is shattered. Naturally, I did what any other mature, responsible adult would do. I ran away to Tijuana and sought help from Jose Cuervo, bought Louis Vuitton knock-offs and got a killer tan.

Ok, not really. But the thought did cross my mind. Instead I turned to those closest to me. My husband was on my side 110%. He listened, hugged, ranted and empathized. That's his job and he's exceptional at it. And I turned to others who had NOT necessarily signed on for this type of work. Aunts, my stepmom, my best gal-pals, sympathetic co-workers. It wasn't that I was calling everyone up and bitching about what had happened. I was asking for coping tips and advice. I was trying to get a handle on how to get used to the "new normal" of being estranged from my parents.

Now, looking back over the years since that dark, dismal August, I realize I was doing something else. I was finding new mothers.

The two "aunties." Now, you might think from that label that I'm talking about a couple of white-haired ladies wearing floral muumuus and going to Bingo every Tuesday in the recreation room at The Home. Hardly. My two aunts are closer in age to my husband than to my parents and have always been more like sisters to me than aunts. And because of their placement on the family tree, the situation with my parents was a very big part of their lives too. I can only imagine how hard it was for them. They were conflicted over loyalty and trying to be peacemakers. They wanted this worked out. They wanted me to stop crying. While trying not to get in the middle of "IT", they had conversations with my mother and tried to reason with her. They asked her direct questions and they heard answers that were very hard to hear. They advocated for me while being honest and forthright with information that was difficult to swallow. And have I mentioned that neither aunt is biologically related to me. They could have opted out at any time. They didn't.
They remained my best friends, confidants and have healed me more than they know. We laughed together, cried together and even had an occasional disagreement. But they have stood by me and I feel closer to them than ever before. And they never, ever let a conversation end without telling me they loved me.

My stepmom I first met my stepmom when I was 16 and she was 24. Yup, 24 and holding my 6-month-old baby sister. She seemed so mature, exotic and sexy to me. Of course, when you're a 16 year old in the 80s, anyone NOT wearing parachute pants and a banana clip is exotic.

Finally telling her about the emotional Armageddon with my parents, six months after it happened, was both difficult and a huge relief. My stepmother's heart is the size of Jupiter and she just simply doesn't know how to be mean. To anyone. Even if they deserve it. I could feel her take on some of the pain I had been dealing with and make it her own. Which I didn't want her to do but then again, sure I did. I needed her to do exactly what she did, even if I didn't know what I needed at the time.

As the weeks became months, months turned into seasons, the topic was discussed less and less. I heard from her more than I had in the past and she and my father visited more than they ever had. Were they rejoicing and feeling like "ha ha, we win!"? Absolutely not. They were devastated to think that such a lack of forgiveness could exist as a daily part of someone's life. They were saddened to see me being discarded by people I loved.

Ironically, as a result of my relationship with them being "out of the closet" after 22 years, our time together became easier, more relaxed and quite natural. Ok, I'll admit, calling a woman only nine years older than me "stepmom" has never been natural but most people think we're sisters and we just go with that. She listens to me and offers theories that have a unique perspective behind them. She is my father's true soul mate. Mommy to my baby sisters. And she tells me she loves me at the end of every conversation.

The Artists. Psychologists would probably have a lot to say about the fact that my creative juices began to flow, bubble over and flood out of me simultaneous to the upheaval in my family. I had always been crafty and showed a bit of creative flair but suddenly, I was An Artist. I made a bedroom into a studio, began sticking stuff together left and right and the next thing I knew, I was selling my art at shows and by special order. And boy, did I get rich! Financially?? Uh, no. But two women became a part of my life as a result of this art endeavor and have made me wealthy with sisterhood, peace and love. And yes, it is supposed to sound just that hippy-ish because one

of them IS a total hippy and the other is a precious nymph of happiness! These women have brought so much color, humor and inspiration to my spirit that I'm not sure how I got this far without them. And they seem to think I'm pretty groovy too. They buy my stuff, critique my stuff, offer ideas for more stuff, make their own amazing stuff and love all the stuff they surround themselves with. I am learning so much from them about surrounding yourself with the good stuff. Good people, art that makes you happy, the God of your choice, nature, wine, freedom, music, children and dogs. Yes, these things seem obvious don't they? But I promise you, very few people have enough of any one of the above in their life AND appreciate it in a way that enriches them and makes their soul dance. These two whimsical women have nourished places in me that I didn't know existed. Mothers of sons. A breast cancer survivor.
New...*ridiculously young*... grandmothers.
Artists. And I know they love me each time we hug, laugh, celebrate and create.

Gal Pals. Sisterhood of the Traveling Pants. Ya-Ya Sisterhood. Women sure do have a way of giving cute titles to their groups of most intimate girlfriends. But I suppose that the women who are so tightly woven into the fabric of our lives deserve a title. Mine are the Mountain Mommas.

I met one while doing community theatre, one at the wedding of the first, and the third at church. I was in one's wedding and she was in mine. None of us had babies when we met but now there are nine children between us and two who went to heaven. We've added divorce to the list of things we've shared and we've said sad farewells to grandparents and friends. We have been there for each other's tattoos. We've shared breastfeeding issues, Baptisms and birthday parties.

These three women have made me laugh so hard that I have pulled muscles. They have made me cry by the depth of their compassion and the dedication of their love for their children. I can tell them absolutely anything and know that I will not be judged. I also know that they will be honest with me even if our viewpoints differ. The Mountain Mommas have taught me that I can love God, know Jesus and still have a good laugh at a penis joke without worrying about eternal damnation. These are the very girlfriend relationships that men roll their eyes at and cannot comprehend. Yes, we really are THAT close.

There is no other person in our lives like our mothers. They feel our soul's blossom before we take our first breath. They carry a piece of us with them wherever they go. Oddly enough, some of them bail out and are not with us for our entire journey. So be it.

Do these special women that I celebrate in my life replace my mother? No. And that's ok. I wasn't looking for a replacement. I wasn't really looking for anything. And yet, I found mothers. Mothers with extra love that they are more than willing to share. They infused me with it by being exactly who they are supposed to be and loving me unconditionally. Just like a mother should.

Tabatha Renegar

Slow Down and Take the Time

The older I get, the more I realize what the truly important things in life are. The people who have touched my life the most are not those with great power, wealth or fame. Those who take the time to really listen, to show they care, and are there when needed are the ones that mean the most. Slowing down and taking the time to appreciate the people in our lives and the beauty of the world around us brings a special joy. When we stay so busy and rush through life, it's easy to miss opportunities to touch and be touched by others and experience the music and artistry of creation.

Help us to slow down, Lord,
and not to hurry so,
not having to scurry so,
fret, fume and worry so.
Help us to take time
to savor everyday,
to experience the beauty
to be found along our way.
Give us your tranquility,
a quiet, peaceful mind,
taking time so we can find
opportunities to be kind.

Help us to slow down, Lord,

not to rush through every
hour,
to reflect on the power
in the beauty of a flower.
Help us to take time
to really look around
and appreciate the miracles
waiting to be found.
Give us time for quietness
and a listening ear
so life's music we can hear
and be aware that You are
near.

Connie Arnold

Chapter Five

Loss

Say not "Good night," but in some brighter clime,
bid me, "Good morning."

-   Anna Laetitia Barbauld

She Was the Music

"You'll need to decide what to do when the time comes." The doctor's words echoed in my mind as I sat quietly by my mother's bedside. The previous evening, my stepfather and I had been summoned to the hospital's family room to discuss the options. She was rapidly declining; and had no living will. "Do whatever it takes to save her," my stepfather had asserted. "I don't care what it is, just do whatever it takes."

Three days earlier, while I was enjoying what would turn out to be the last time my mom and I would spend time alone together, the oncologist on call paid a visit to her hospital room to give us the results of her total body CT scan and brain MRI. The news was not good. We had both gotten used to getting bad news over the past year, but neither of us expected the news we received. The cancer had metastasized to her liver and brain. They could use radiation to pinpoint the two tumors on her brain. Additional chemotherapy would presumably zap the tumors on her liver. For months now, she had undergone chemo drug after chemo drug tirelessly fighting the tiny tumors that riddled her spine and lungs all to no avail. The pain was unbearable for her yet she still managed to keep a smile on her face. I was her biggest concern. *She* didn't want *me* to have to go through this.

After the doctor left the room, Mom and I talked for hours about living and dying. She was going to fight like hell; but if she didn't make it through this she wanted me to know that she was at peace with God. She told me what she wanted for her funeral. Lots of music. No special requests; she would leave that to me. She had filled my childhood with music and trusted my tastes. She told me how proud she was that I was her daughter. I told her that I was the one who was proud.

Over the next couple of days, the brain tumors took over my lovely mom's body and mind. She lost her motor functions and was unable to perform the simplest of tasks. She screamed in pain while I frantically begged the doctor to administer morphine. After the morphine pump was started, she slept until the fog began to lift, then she reached for her head, eyes closed, a pained expression on her face, unable to push the button. I stayed by her side night and day, pushing the button every time she reached for her head and changing her cold compress after every dose.

"You'll need to decide what to do when the time comes." The doctor spoke of a brain shunt used to pour chemo drugs directly onto her brain. He explained the available life-saving measures, clinically informing us that chest compressions would likely crush her ribs, causing great pain and possibly puncturing a lung. He confirmed that she would never walk again as a result of the tumor pressing on her spinal cord. She had, at best, a couple of months.

At around 4 am on August 7, as I was changing the cold compress, my mom opened her eyes for the last time. "I love you, Mom" I whispered to her. At that moment, a big, glorious smile came over her beautiful face. It was the smile that had comforted me for my entire life and I looked into her bright blue eyes and smiled back, caressing her face. She closed her eyes and drifted back to sleep. She died at 9 pm that night as I was holding her hand. I watched her take her last breath and felt her heartbeat stumble, then stop. "She's gone." I whispered. "We need to call the doctor!" my stepfather urged as he stood, heading for the door. "Let her go." I quietly responded. He stopped and sat back down. "What if…" he trailed off. "We need to let her go." I repeated.

In that moment of my mother's death, I realized that I had to do what was right for her. It was the most important decision of my life. She had been full of life and light – a person who exemplified *joie de vivre*. She had *lived* and lived well. A shunt, broken ribs, a wheelchair – those were not meant for her. She was meant to dance and sing and play and love. She *was* the music she loved to hear; and she was at peace with God. It was time to let her go.

Jennifer Chapman Brooks

A Mother's Strength

My story is one of my mom, the lessons that she taught me while she was on this earth, and the strength that she continues to bring me from Heaven.

My mom, Mary, was the mother of 11 children and loved each one of us as though we each were her favorite. My mom and dad's marriage ended when eight of us were still in high school or younger. I remember so clearly how my mom cried, day and night, and we would kneel by her bed soothing her and telling her how much we loved her. I prayed hard at her bedside for God to bless her with the strength that I knew was in her, that she needed especially at that time. From that day on, I have no doubt that God answers prayers!

Part of this strength was Mom's ability to empower her children to be a working part of the family. We always attended Mass together and grew closer as brothers and sisters than we ever thought possible. She worked tirelessly as our mom and as the breadwinner of the family. She taught us how important it was to work and give back. Times were very tight, but by the grace of God, we all went to Catholic school where lessons from home were reinforced. My mom was a piano teacher and music teacher, and she even worked as a hostess at McDonald's to help us be the people we are today. My mom put into action the words of Pope Benedict XVI, *"The family is the privileged setting where every person learns to give and receive love...The family is also a school which enables men and women to grow to the full measure of their humanity."* She was truly amazing.

I prayed by her bedside as a teenager and then again as an adult in her final days on this earth. How I wanted God to let me take her place, but He had other plans. One night, before I went to bed, I said "Good night" to my mom and whispered in her ear that we would be okay. I told her I would continue to rely on God to help me carry on the traditions of this family that she built with her love, her strength, her faith, and her perseverance. My sister woke me up early the next morning and let me know that my mom had passed from this life.

So, to this day, I tell my mom "Good night," and ask God to continue to bless me with the strength and commitment to family that He blessed my mom with. I thank Him for blessing me with a family that continues to grow through my mom's love.

Gabrielle Noyes

One Breath at a Time

Months ago I thought about submitting an essay for a contest in a magazine, and the topic was, "When did you first know love?" In the Socratic way, I must first define love before I can admit to the full recognition of this word that connotes grace and beauty.

Looking into my mother's sea-blue eyes, I told her that I would take time off and come home to help her recover from yet another bout of COPD (chronic obstructive pulmonary disease)…that we would take things a day at a time. Mom replied in her breathless raspy voice, "Honey, I can only live one <u>breath</u> at a time."

I knew she was dying, but was sad for myself. God had blessed her with six children and her place was soon to be with Him. Devoutly religious, Mom had knelt at her bedside each night and thanked God for her children; today she was grateful to have the strength to live one more day waiting for my sisters Leslie and Donna to arrive.

Love is what we do. Failing health never hindered my mother's resolve; it only altered her pace. With the arrival of each grandchild, Mom traveled to each of our homes from Chicago to Atlanta caring for 13 grandchildren as well as the parents. Preparing three meals daily, meticulous house cleaning, folding mountains of laundry, even organizing the "catch-all" drawer in the kitchens, Mom gave us all specific instructions on the proper way to change a diaper and dress a newborn baby. In fact, she gave my son, Jeff, his first bath. Fussing at me to return to bed, Mom demonstrated the fastest newborn bath on record.

To date, I can still remember Mom walking up my hardwood stairs, one slow step at a time, breathing heavily, carrying trays of food. The years of smoking left her short of breath with any exertion, yet every day she cooked and brought me meals and ended up staying a month. In January of 1996, Mom returned, ready to cook, clean and care for Laura Catherine, the last of her 13 grandchildren. After receiving a call from me telling her that I needed an urgent cesarean section to deliver Laura, she made my father drop everything at his law practice and drive five hours to Winston-Salem. Mom didn't skip a beat and moved into our home caring for every detail and everyone. She was love in action.

Less than 17 months later, I received a phone call late one night from my dad saying that my mother was being stubborn and refused to let him take her to the emergency department. I insisted on seeing her, telling Dad to say I was getting into my car to drive to Williamson, West Virginia. She said she would agree to go to the Emergency Department if I agreed to stay home.

Immediately, I called my brothers and sisters saying I was leaving within a half-hour - something in her weak voice told me this illness was different. I arrived at the hospital at 4 a.m. and reminded Mom that I was just as strong-willed as she. Mom's determined spirit remained strong in spite of her rapidly declining body, and she found the strength to live until all of her children were at her side. Mom had made it clear she did not want to be on a respirator, so our decision was to bring her home where she passed away in the same bed where she had said countless prayers of gratitude, surrounded by all of her children.

As my mom took her last breath, I experienced an epiphany: the person who loved me most unconditionally had passed. Acutely, I was aware of the nature of God's love also: unconditional. Love was my mom in action, caring for others more than herself, giving her time and energy in abundance without expectation. During my life, this love had not been fully recognized until she took her last breath. Love is unconditional; it's what you do, one breath at a time.

Cindy Ward Brasher

Be Inspired

Our tender moments with our loved ones at the end are the times we never forget... we never want to forget...but I truly believe these experiences are what make us who we are. We choose to move on and be a little gentler, a little kinder, a little more compassionate, better listeners, more understanding of one another, and we end up wanting to be more like the ones we lose so others can see them alive within us.

Rene Noyes Bauwens

***

Death is nothing at all.

It does not count.

I have only slipped away into the next room. Nothing has happened.

Everything remains exactly as it was.

I am I, and you are you, and the old life that we lived so fondly

together is untouched, unchanged.

Whatever we were to each other that we are still.

by Henry Scott Holland ~ 1847-1918
Canon of St. Paul's Cathedral ~ London. UK

Acknowledgements

I am so grateful to all of the women who participated in this project. I began this book over six years ago, but it was put on the back burner on more than one occasion. Sometimes it was life's circumstances; sometimes it was my own procrastination. There came a point when I couldn't have this book sit around anymore, because I wanted to make sure the stories that had been given to me were heard. So here we are.

Special thanks to my biggest cheerleaders on this project: my mom, Mary Jo Brown Thompson, for always being in my corner; my dad, John Hash, for always encouraging me and sharing this book journey with me; to my wise women from Bible study at St. Paul's, my Book Club girlfriends and my Mountain Mommas.

Thanks also to Polly Cogar Bowman who gave me advice on organization of the book's topics and purpose early on in the project; to Christine Pomper, who implored me to stick with it and gave me my first deadline; to Colleen Pierce Lopina who helped with editing and made me rethink how to say what I needed to say; to Bonnie Davis for her 21st century editing expertise, and to Aly Goodwin Gregg for her marketing advice.

Appendix

A variety of topics have been touched on in the book. If you or someone you know might need help, here are some resources:

Alcoholics-anonymous.com
This website can help you locate meetings for AA as well as Al-Anon, Children of Alcoholics, Ala-Teen meetings, etc.

National Suicide Prevention hotline:
1-800-273-TALK (8255)

National Sexual Assault hotline:
1-800-656-HOPE (4673)

Childhelp National Abuse hotline:
1-800-4-A-CHILD

Bibliography

Bronte, Charlotte. *Jane Eyre,* Smith, Elder and Company, Cornhill, 1847.

Julian, of Norwich. *Revelations of Divine Love,* 1495.

Book of Common Prayer, p. 640, (Seabury Press, New York, 1979.)

"I am not afraid..." Joan of Arc, born circa 1412.

Baily, Philip James. "Festus: A Poem," Boston, 1853.

"A River Runs Through It" © 1992 Allied Filmmakers, N.V. All rights reserved. Courtesy of Columbia Pictures.

The Works of Anna Laetitia Barbauld: With a memoir, Volume 1, edited by Lucy Aikin, Copyright © 2014 in this compilation Cambridge University Press. Reprinted with the permission of Cambridge University Press.

Cannon Henry Scott Holland. *Death is Nothing at All*, London, England, 1910.

About the Editor

Elizabeth Hash Lopina grew up in West Virginia and is a graduate of Xavier University in Cincinnati, Ohio. She lives in Winston-Salem, North Carolina with her husband and three children.

www.ingramcontent.com/pod-product-compliance
Lightning Source LLC
Chambersburg PA
CBHW071637050426
42443CB00028B/3371